A Royal Diadem
and
Leaves of the Tree

Other Writings by Walter Lanyon

Abd Allah, Teacher, Healer
A Lamp unto My Feet
And It Was Told of a Certain Potter
Behold the Man ◆ Embers
The Eyes of the Blind
I Came ◆ The Impatient Dawn
Impressions of a Nomad
It Is Wonderful ◆ The Joy Bringer
The Laughter of God
A Light Set upon a Hill
London Notes and Lectures
Out of the Clouds
Quintology: Ask and Ye Shall Receive
A Royal Diadem *and* Leaves of the Tree
That Ye Might Have
The Temple Not Made with Hands
Thrust in the Sickle
Treatment *and* Demonstration *and* Your Heritage
Without the Smell of Fire

Available through:
Mystics of the World
Eliot, Maine
www.mysticsoftheworld.com

A Royal Diadem
and
Leaves of the Tree

Walter C. Lanyon

A Royal Diadem
and
Leaves of the Tree

Mystics of the World First Edition 2017
Published by Mystics of the World
ISBN-10:1-946362-08-5
ISBN-13:978-1-946362-08-7

For information contact:

Mystics of the World
Eliot, Maine
www.mysticsoftheworld.com

Cover graphics by Margra Muirhead
Printed by CreateSpace
Available from Mystics of the World and Amazon.com

Walter C. Lanyon, 1887–1967

Contents

A Royal Diadem
- You Sent that Letter this Morning, Didn't You? 9
- Realization 11
- Your Talent 14
- I Am That Which I Desire to Be 17
- Camilla 19
- Before the Sandman Comes 22
- My Cup Runneth Over 24
- The Other Fellow 26
- A Divided Kingdom 29
- Let There Be Light 32

Leaves of the Tree
- Failure to Demonstrate 37
- Letting Go 43
- Cast Your Bread upon the Waters 51
- God 53
- As a Man Thinketh 58
- Invisible Power 61
- Think on These Things 65
- The Lord is Mindful of His Own 67
- Your Problem 69
- Oneness 76
- Reversing 84

About the Author 93

A Royal Diadem

You Sent that Letter this Morning, Didn't You?

You carefully wrote it, addressed and sealed it, and then you dropped it in the box. You didn't have a string tied to it, did you? No, you just dropped it in the box and went on your way. You didn't think that the box was especially burglar-proof, did you? And you didn't wonder how it would get from the box to the post office, and from the post office to the train, did you? You didn't spend all that morning worrying about whether the train would arrive with it, did you? No, you dropped it lightheartedly into the box and forgot it.

You sent that prayer this morning, didn't you? You carefully made your declarations for right and offset the wrong thoughts. You addressed your prayer to the All Highest and Only One. But what did you do after you had sent it? You had a string of worry attached to it and kept pulling it back to you to see if you could not add another word, or to see if it were really "made." All morning long you doubted, and at evening you still doubted, and the next morning you sent another prayer; but it too was attached by a string of doubt and fear and did not get far.

Several days after you sent the letter, you received an answer which read: "I have your letter of such and such a date," and you recalled that you had written a letter. Still, you didn't rush outdoors and stop every passerby and say, "I sent a letter and got a reply" and then elaborate on how you went through the whole affair; how you had hunted for paper and spilled the ink, or lost your pencil, etc. No, you accepted the letter, read it, got the benefit from it, and went on your way. And finally in a half-hearted way, the poor little prayer, which was only half loosened, came back to you with a ray of light, and you rushed to your nearest neighbor and said, "I had a demonstration—you see, it was this way ...."

"O ye of little faith!" Why don't you cut the strings of worry that are attached to your every thought and "loose it and let it go?" Have the same faith back of your prayer that you have back of the letter, and it will return to you with greater certainty and with surer reward.

Away out in the front lines while the battle was raging, a carrier pigeon was let loose with a message, and as he disappeared into the distance, fading away into the limpid blue of the sky, no worried thought hampered his voyage. When they "loosed him and let him go," they knew that he would fly to his destination and results would follow.

Who has not felt the perfect faith of a child in St. Nicholas? They ask for their heart's desire and are never left without some expression of love. When you ask, ask as believing, and you shall receive. You don't go into a store and ask the clerk for a certain article and then chase madly about, repeating the request a thousand times. You ask and then wait. So when we learn to ask and wait—wait with the patience which is absolute faith—then we shall constantly receive the reply, the reward that is rightfully ours.

"Ask, and ye shall receive; seek, and ye shall find; knock, and it shall be opened unto you." Don't knock and at the same time try to force an entrance by the window. The master of the house will take you for a robber and only bar his doors heavier. And so, as you send a letter, send your prayers—let them go forth unhampered, untrammeled by fear, worry, or care. Don't stampede your thoughts. A multitude of assertions accomplishes nothing; it only congests your thinking. Speak to your Father in secret, and He will reward thee openly.

Realization

Stop waiting and start realizing: all things are possible to the man who believes and who trusts in God. You don't have to wait for the kingdom of heaven until you die. You cannot die into it, and long years of waiting will not bring it any nearer, for "the kingdom of heaven is at hand." *Now* is your keynote—stop living in the future and get into the *now* of your life.

Wherever this finds you, look about you and see what percent of your life you really live in waiting, expecting something that is coming, never grasping the idea that it is all here right now.

Act as possessing all things. Jesus' mission on Earth was to set aside all old ideas of material growth. He didn't have to spend long years digging in the mountains to find gold with which to pay his taxes. He turned to the illimitable Source of supply which was at hand to bless, and drew his substance, his gold. He did not have to plant wheat, cultivate it, and worry along with it in order to have bread to feed the multitude. He just reached out into the storehouse of the all-present Mind and realized that it was the substance of all things and that what he needed to do was to realize it.

He realized all things and always acknowledged their presence before they were seen with the material eye. For we read that he "raised his eyes to heaven (centered his attention on the inexhaustible Source) and gave thanks." Yes, he gave thanks before he could see it. Why? Because he knew that God is the source of all there is and that He abundantly supplied His ideas with that which was needful. Not gold in the desert, where there was nothing to buy, but water. The mind of God is logical—It is logic.

It works in rhythm, in cadence, and never loses or gains in action but is a steady, perpetual motion.

"God's in His heaven—all's right with the world!" ... "The kingdom of heaven is at hand" ... "The kingdom of heaven is within you." Only believe, and all things are yours. "Now is the accepted time"—right now, while you are reading this. Right now while I am writing is the accepted time to bring about realization, to live it, to sing it, to go about our Father's business, using His inexhaustible supply. Absence of God in our thoughts is the only thing that can keep away demonstration. Where God is, there is an abundance of all things—He feeds us on His ideas.

You think you lack love, money, home, etc., but what you really lack is the consciousness of God. If He were dwelling in your thoughts continually, these things would be added. Jesus did not worry about hotel accommodations when he went from place to place. He simply knew that the upper chamber was always ready for him. All things are mental before they are expressed in the material. Then speak the word out: "My word shall not return unto me void, but shall accomplish whereunto it is sent." What a wonderful command to leave with us, and he has said that "the things I do, ye shall do also, and even greater." He spoke the word to the sea, and it was calm; he spoke supply to tangible existence; he spoke health to light—and "the things I do, ye shall do also."

Wake up your realization. Make it part of your daily task to realize things for right now. Act as possessing all things. "When ye pray, believe that ye shall have these things." The Bible is vibrant with help and instructions for the *now*-ness of our lives—constantly are we invited to live now.

Start realization to work today. Realize that you have God's love with you right now, and as you grow from step to step, you will see "the word made flesh." You will feel the thrill of this present *Presence*. Keep saying to yourself, "Now is the accepted time; now is the day of salvation." There is no material law that can hold you back. The way is clear, and the open door is through this consciousness of realization.

Your Talent

Did you know that you have a special something, a special, peculiar little something that makes you different from the whole world? Of course you did. But you never dreamed that it would enable you to step out of the ugly, gray mass of routine living and give you a little place all of your own. No, I don't mean that it would make a queen or a mighty monarch of you, but it will make you infinitely greater, and this little something that lies wrapped in the napkin of fear and which you only visit in the very secret closet of your own imagination is your talent.

You've been so used to fading out of sight and being a member of those who accept all things that you never even made an effort to see what you would really be like if you "cut loose" once and let this little seed in you take root and flower.

In your heart of hearts is written your name—a name which is peculiar to you and which no other idea has—and it is this name, this something, which is to be brought out, to be made great.

Mariah was from far-off Russia. She worked hard in the fields with her sisters and brothers, but something kept whispering to her. Something within stirred. It was talent, which was working itself out of the napkin. It pointed the way out across the land far across the seas into a strange place that she knew not of, but a fearlessness led her on, and every day the way was made clearer, until at last she found herself in her place—a place which was waiting for her in a land where few spoke her tongue. But that place was hers and the talent led her to it, and it was a place of growth and success, of happiness and harmony.

Your Talent

So within you, the talent keeps whispering and trying to edge its way out of the napkin of your fear, but you keep wrapping it tighter with new illusions and will not let it come to the light. You are afraid to do what it bids you do. "What would people say?" You are overcome with the fear that other people would say things. They intimidate you into a state of "grayness." You don't dare to come out and be yourself.

You coward! You are afraid to live your life, the life that you cherish above all things. You are scared to become great because it means work, and it means hewing to the line and letting the world take care of itself. Let them talk—their gossiping and sneers will soon be turned into hero worship. They are the "gray mass" to which you belonged and they change with the wind. Don't mind them when they say, "You cannot" or, "Aren't you afraid to do that?" These very voices will be saying, "I always knew that you would make a go of it."

Here's what you need: more communion with God. Take Him at His word and trust Him to the last letter of His promises. He wants to bless you—to manifest Himself through you, to make your talent shine forth—and He's the only partner you need in life's business. You need Him and you need His instructions. "Get wisdom." Wisdom comes from cutting away from the worldly things and turning your attention to Love—childlike (not childish) and simple.

Your place is waiting for you. It is the place of your desires, if your desires are good. It is beckoning you, and God is willing to lead you there and to call you by the secret name which is written in the tablet of your heart.

Can't you just let go? Can't you just break away from all the old things and plunge forth, guided by this talent, this name, and live your own life? By so doing, you will be losing your material sense of life and find that which is real, that which is eternal and lasting. When the material napkin which is holding your talent from the light is taken away, then you are wrapped in the substance of Mind, which is infinite and in which you can go on unfolding, growing grander, nobler, and lovelier each succeeding year.

I Am That Which I Desire to Be

Do you know the secret of life? Do you know the password which will open all closed doors? Do you know the thrill of real life? Would you like to feel continually as you do on some fine spring morning, when the sun is just peeping through the rose and turquoise and flirting with a million diamond dewdrops?

You can. Here is the password for you: *I am that which I desire to be.*

One moment, please. Use no headstrong, blind and stubborn willpower. Use no struggling, mental gymnastics and contort your mind by vainly declaring so many words.

Listen:

You remember who I AM THAT I AM is, don't you? It is the name of every living man. Because I AM has sent me. My name is I AM. Your name is I AM.

What did I AM send you here for but to give expression to Himself; to give expression to love, beauty, holiness, harmony, happiness. Take your Bible down from the shelf and find out what the attributes of God are. They are peace, holiness, happiness, beauty.

Your means of communication with God is called prayer, and prayer is desire. Doesn't it begin to look simple? You have your I AM and your meaning for "desire." And since all good comes from God, who is good, then even your desires are in reality the "still small voice" seeking utterance in you. Yes, your very desires are in reality, insofar as they are good, the open lines of communication—the messages from God to you.

Did you ever desire to be that which you are not? Did you ever desire to be strong, well, happy, and well-supplied? Aren't these all good desires? Where did they come from? From the base so-called mortal mind?

You never stopped to realize, did you, that your desires are the embryonic formations waiting to be made manifest in the flesh. "Thy will be done." Let Thyself be manifested in me.

"As a man thinketh in his heart, so is he." What are you thinking?

"Now are we the sons of God"—*now*, in great, glowing, vibrant letters. No matter what you were an hour or a minute or even a year ago, *now* are we the sons of God. *Now*—think about the present possibility of the word—*now*.

The pattern which molds our desires is already cast for us Sons of God. Then desire to be what you are—a child of the King. Are you acting to the full extent of your nobility? "Seek (in prayer, desire) the kingdom of heaven (which is within), and all things shall be added."

All things are yours. You are that which you desire to be—*now*.

Camilla

Camilla is not a storybook character. She is not a creature manufactured to suit the issue. She is a real, live woman, a nun, living in an old, gray stone convent situated on a beautiful mountain which overlooks the winding Moselle River.

We met her one morning, coming from the little chapel where she had been at prayer. It was a clear morning with a high blue sky; the faint perfume of wild mountain flowers and vegetation was in the air—the year was at spring. As she stepped out into the open, she seemed to fit perfectly with the setting, as if she were the personification of youth eternal. As she passed us, she did not shyly cast her eyes to the ground but looked up at us with wide-open blue eyes—eyes full of lovely fearlessness; eyes full of depth and wonder; eyes of youth with the wisdom of ages shining through them. This woman had youth in her grasp—clear, firm, white skin with a transparency to it; lips red and full of expression. Youth was so evident that it made itself felt.

"Not a minute over eighteen," said one of us. But Camilla was a woman who would soon count her years sixty. Later in the day, I talked with her, and here is how she did it.

"At twenty, I found myself practically an old woman, both in mind and body. I was weary; life was more or less a burden to me, and it was at this time I became a nun. Soon after I began to study 'the Word' it came to me that I had never really lived; that the sense of fleeting youth which I had was nothing but a shadow, a shadow of the real youth which was eternal and everlasting. I soon realized that God could not grow old, not in the sense of decay; that nature never grew old—she renewed herself annually—and gradually I came to know that if God could not grow old, that Man, His idea and image and likeness, could not age.

"In seeking the kingdom of heaven first, we are told that all things shall be added to us. In seeking the kingdom of heaven, we are seeking youth, joy, harmony, happiness. The kingdom is not made up of aged persons. It is vibrant with youth eternal. And finally I began to realize that I was a part of the kingdom of heaven and that in reality I was only seeking my true Self.

"'Seek and ye shall find; knock and it shall be opened unto you; ask and ye shall receive.' So I went forth seeking the real life. As God was everywhere present, I found Him expressed in all nature. I found Him expressed in His universe—and I was of His universe. In fact, I was a part of it—not a part *from* it. Just like the lovely force which impelled the rose to cover her vines with snowy white blossoms, I found that power growing and growing in me, swelling up in me, until one day I felt the complete thrill—the divine spark—which awakened in me and made me feel this rejuvenation taking place.

"God is everywhere, and He is life eternal and youth eternal. If He is eternal youth and is everywhere, I could literally bathe in youth. Not only that, but I felt that I was a part of the whole scheme and drew my life, my vitality, my youth from the same source which impelled the whole plan. Yonder on the mountain, the gray mist hovered and swayed over the crest. The sun plunged through it, and then the blue patch showed in the distance. The heather on the foothills was like a flash of purple; the white hawthorn tree glistened in the warm sun, and I, a part of it, vibrated with youth eternal.

"I learned to love it all—love the whole plan like one loves the members of his own household. Nothing was unlovely when viewed rightly, and everything yielded to the touch of its gentleness—the touch of love. If it rained, I went about my duties with a feeling that everything was being purified, that everything was being filled full of purity, and I too drank deeply of purity. If the sun poured down upon me, I felt it making a halo about me of pure gold—gold that would endure. I felt it sifted joy all about me and filled the throats of the birds with glorious notes, and so I sang and thrilled for life. If the wind blew and raged about, I was happy yet in the thought that things were being changed about. This was a readjustment; old dead leaves were caught up and carried off, dust was moved from secluded corners. Readjustment was taking place, and so I felt the readjustment enter me, the power to say, 'Not mine, but thine be done.' In winter, when the snow fell, I knew that everything in this universe was busily engaged working and studying, unfolding and getting ready for greater growth.

"So I learned from the weather that, after all, it was but for a lesson to us—that we should rejoice regardless what the manifestation was. Further, I began to realize that not only was I seeking youth, happiness harmony, but that I *was* youth, happiness, harmony."

Just then a band of happy youngsters came running up the hill and caught Camilla in their arms, grabbing onto her long black skirts. Youth had sought youth and found it and bore her off down into the flower-dotted valley. Camilla was sixty—the world called her sixteen.

Before the Sandman Comes

Did you ever invite the sandman over to see you and have him turn you down? Or have you ever waked up in the night and found that half a dozen long, never-ending, black hours were awaiting you before morning would come? I know you have, and I know that sometimes you have tried that old trick of self-hypnotism, counting the sheep as they went over the fence, and found that it too failed, and at last in sheer despair you have tossed and tumbled about and mentally flayed yourself into a state of absolute fatigue.

Did you know that there was a sure and direct way leading into slumberland? So easy to travel, so inviting and interesting; strewn along the way with drowsy, nodding poppies and heavy-scented white lilies, and ever so often a nodding little sleepyhead child all cuddled up so comfy and securely in its mother's arms, and presently such a happy, snuggly feeling comes to you that you let go and tumble off the cliff of dreams into the land of forgetfulness. Let me show you that road.

When you wake, always remember that "I shall be satisfied, when I awake, with thy likeness." What is that likeness? One of its attributes is love, so we will start with that. When I awake in Thy (Love's) likeness, I shall be satisfied. You are already awake in an atmosphere of Love, for in Him you "live and move and have your being." Now, the way to bring this Love into your mind is to put it into use—start loving—and to do this you begin forgiving.

Forgive Mr. X that little resentment which you hold against him, and Mrs. Blank the hurt that you received from her words. Take them by the hand and lead them out through "green pastures" and "beside still waters." Say to them, "I forgive you; I have nothing in my heart against you, nothing in my heart against anybody, for I love the whole world." Such a feeling will come to you, such a contented, peaceful feeling, and you will be all aglow with the flame of real Love.

Finally, as you go on your way forgiving, you will come to your own poor self standing there—that poor old dear which you have so hatefully accused of all sorts of wrongs of sickness, sin, and death. You have fastened all these things on it, and it needs to be forgiven too. "Neither do I condemn thee; go, and sin no more." Now you have loosed everything, even your own self, and no wonder you lie there and radiate and radiate love.

At last, as you ponder the wonders of Love and the thrill of forgiveness, you will feel the soft feathers of His wings folding about you. They will hover over you and "the everlasting arms" will take you up ever so gently. With your head snugly nestled against your Father's breast, you will be borne off into that haven of rest and shall arise therefrom, glowing with newness of life and purpose.

So the next time the sandman won't come to see you, try this plan of forgiving the whole world and see if a sweeter sense of peace does not come to you than you have ever experienced before.

A tired and worn-out soldier boy tried this one dark night, when it seemed that the enemy was pretty thick and that they were pretty near and doing their best to keep him awake. But when he walked with them through green pastures and beside still waters and when he anointed their heads with the oil of forgiveness, the noise of the guns didn't matter anymore; the unrest and fear all faded away, and he went over the cliff of dreamland.

My Cup Runneth Over

"Thou anointest my head with oil; my cup runneth over," sang the psalmist. The cup of our desire is to be filled with joy—not only filled, but filled to running over. The cup of our desire is a complete willingness to let God enter your life and there have full sway.

"The Lord is in his holy temple" ... "Let all the earth rejoice." And then we read that the temple is the body. Now, the Lord is in the midst of us. He is in our very midst and is filling the cup of our desire to the brim and running it over.

Like the mountain spring rushes, gushes down the mountainsides, fills the basin full—yes, full to overflowing—and the surplus waters the valley beneath, so God is filling our hearts with the spontaneous, life-giving joy which, when we let it run over on all sides, blesses and heals all who come in contact with it.

It's an impersonal matter. You let your cup be so full of joy and take no thought where it is going to run over. Everything in the universe thrives on joy. Even your dog knows when the joy is running over, because you meet him with a dash, with a snap, and he responds with the same joy. Your best friend responds immediately to your joy. He slaps you on the back or puts his arm over your shoulder; he is happy to see you, to bask for a while in your joy. The child in the street greets you with the smile you give it. The man in the street feels helped by your joy. Let your joy be so spontaneous; let it flow; let it burst up in the midst of a desert of gloom and see its oily, soothing effect on the crowd.

You have a reason to be happy. There is a reason for the faith which is within you. Floodtides of love are open to you, constantly flowing to you, and you are but the channel, open and free for it to pass through. Then relax, let go of the stiff, formal life where you are always under a mask, afraid of public opinion, afraid that something will happen if you let yourself be natural. Sure, something will happen, and that something is that you will find yourself a new creature in Christ Jesus—the new mind will be in you. The new name will be written upon your forehead, and ye shall be called blessed.

Hatred cannot stand the power of joy; a joyful man can outwit and overcome it at every turn in the road. Anger is turned aside by joy. Sin is blasted and withered in the presence of this holy substance, for it finds not its pleasure in the senses but in right doing, in clear thinking and in purity. Real joy is born of purity. Its motive power is right doing—it glories in the fact that it is reflecting the Word that it is in reality "the Word made flesh." It goes about its work singing, not a foolish little ditty but a lofty psalm of praise which is more felt than heard.

So in the morning, when you turn over for that last forty winks, just have a little talk with your "friend" self and decide to begin the day with joy. See if you cannot get that full-to-overflowing feeling in your heart. Let it gush up in you, that great feeling:

> I am one with God. I am one with the very source of joy. I can go about my work with the real song on my lips and in my heart. I will flood everywhere that I go with light and joy, like the sun floods the Earth.

"Still, still with thee, when purple morning breaketh"—always with God. No matter where you make your bed, you turn hell into heaven because you know "if I make my bed in hell, thou art there," and where God is, is heaven.

He has anointed your head with oil. Your cup is running over with joy—you are joy. Then go forth and give to the starving world. Fill all their vessels full of the blessed substance.

The Other Fellow

"I can't help it," said the young student, with a bitter wave of self-pity. "While I want to do the right thing, the other fellow always wants to do the wrong. While I wouldn't deal unjustly with anyone, knowingly, yet the other fellow seems to take a keen pride in getting by with all sorts of injustices."

Did you ever come to this place? Did you ever seem to stand in this fellow's shoes—that while you loved, you believed that the other fellow hated? That while you lived in accordance with your highest knowledge of truth, you manifested all sorts of ailments while the other fellow went gaily along with perfect health? That while you studied and prayed to be Christlike, you believed that the other fellow derived all the benefits; that he received the things you wanted and needed?

Of course you have, and you have also believed that while you were more or less righteous (that is, at least you desire to be) your path was beset with thorns, while the other fellow trod along a path of roses and "lived by the way," indulging in all sorts of worldly pleasures.

Then you have wondered and wondered why, and right here a great big wedge of despair would force its way into your mind and make you blue and unhappy.

Suppose two men started to build houses side by side, and one of them would drive a nail and then hurry and look around to see what the other was doing, and because he saw the other making a move which he considered false, he would finally get so that his gaze was constantly on the other fellow. He would whack away at his own house without looking to see where he drove his nails. True, after a time he would be able to drive a nail reasonably well without looking at it, but a good many other errors would creep into the construction while he was watching the other fellow make what he called "some mistake." At nightfall, he would be not only physically fatigued but would be a mental wreck as well because he had spent the day assuming one of the most important of duties—and at the same time a forbidden one—that of judging.

God has lovingly relieved you of this unpleasant duty. You don't have to judge anything or anybody, for He takes care of this and rewards accordingly. "Judge not after appearances." How often it seems that something is being entirely destroyed, when only a way is being made for something much more wonderful and better. The breaking of the tiny blue shell of the robin's egg does not spell disaster, as might be thought from the appearances; no, it is an evidence of greater progress. So it is with man; often the thing that is taking place in him, the development which is going on, is a tearing down, a reconstruction which seems grossest error to us.

Get real busy looking within, for there you will find the kingdom of heaven, and forget the other fellow insofar as criticism is concerned. Put him entirely out of your mind and spend your time getting the napkin (mortal bondage) off your own talent so that it can come to light and grow.

Listen! "Ye shall be like a tree planted by the side of a river"—a great, majestic, swaying tree, sweeping the water's edge and touching the sky. Out yonder the mushroom may spring into prominence in a single day, while you are yet a struggling twig. Your growth may be slow and even tiresome at times, but when a little flurry of mortal mind takes place, when a little rain descends, the mushroom topples over and drops into the dust, and you are helped on by these storms. They strengthen you and make you cling closer to the real principle of life.

After a while in your growth, you sit for some sunny moment and look back and remember only faintly the little mushroom which so troubled you. Long ago it passed into oblivion. Long ago it fell into the dust, and you smile inwardly that you ever bothered to wonder why and be discouraged because it seemed to be getting all the benefits and you doing all the work.

You want to take with you this little word: "Judge not from appearances." Let the other fellow develop through whatever lines seem best for him. You are concerned only in helping him when you can. You can let him unfold in the particular way that is best for him, for "He watching over Israel neither slumbers nor sleeps" and is the only true Judge.

A Divided Kingdom

That little kingdom that you call your very own—look at it, examine into it. Is it divided? Are you of one mind and that one the mind that was also in Christ Jesus?

Do you believe that some people love while others hate you? If you do, then your kingdom is divided. Love and hate cannot mingle. There is no common basis for them to meet on, and they cannot dwell in the same kingdom without causing strife, turmoil, and finally a division in the kingdom. If you endow that man with a power to hate you, what good is it for you to say to yourself, "There is naught but love?" What good for you to say, "Love is all-powerful?" Your kingdom is divided and it will fall. Perhaps it will not be utterly cast down, but it will be at strife. Enemies are not for the purpose of retarding your growth but to aid you to cling closer and closer to this great, all-absorbing Love which heals everything, even so-called hate.

Do you believe that matter is the original creator? Do you think the original sin, which is the very foundation of the lie that life is in matter, hence creation is matter, possible? If you do, your kingdom is divided, and what good is it, or what profiteth it for you to declare the nothingness of matter?

Do you believe that Love is both spiritual and sensual and say to yourself, "Suffer it to be so now?" If you do, your kingdom is divided and will fall. It will be of little merit or profit to say there is no sin and that it has no power, while you are indulging the senses. The divided kingdom will tell its own tale when it lies in a heap in the dust.

Do you believe in sickness to the extent that certain things are more difficult than others; that there are so-called stubborn cases which do not yield at once? Do you believe in this and also try to believe that God is health and that He is ever-present and that He is all-powerful? Then the divided power will finally cleave to one of your arguments, and in your direst need, who shall say that it will not be to the belief in stubborn cases.

Do you believe that you have to probe deep into the minds of the wayfarer and find out all his little personal secrets in order to pronounce some certain thing the cause of his trouble? This isn't love, but a morbid curiosity which is hiding behind the veneer of truth which you hold up to your patient. Soon the divided kingdom will no longer be a storehouse of the word of God but a storehouse, or a madhouse, of little petty, personal secrets about this one and that.

Your kingdom is the ever-present *Now*, flowing with milk and honey, a place of light and joy. It is the sheepfold with open doors by which all may go in and out with perfect assurance that therein they will find healing waters and green pastures of rest and strength.

Set the walls of your kingdom to the line—make its four walls true to the standard laid down in the Book. You can do this—start today, by taking a positive stand for God. Build daily with words of love and light. Fill the well of your heart with love; let it overflow so that the thirsty may drink freely. For every error which you have been telling and repeating, start a word of truth in its stead.

Every time you want to utter an unkind word, stop a moment and find one of your soldiers who is on the side of good and send him out. Good words are the soldiers who are fighting on the side of right and bad words the soldiers of darkness. When you bring out a whole battalion of these wicked soldiers and turn them loose in your attempt to picture your brother, you are throwing all your weight in the balance of evil. Words are the expression of thoughts. So many bad words represent so many bad thoughts and vice versa. If you will try for a single day to use nothing but your good soldiers—don't even allow a bad soldier to show himself, let alone be used—you will find that by noon of the first day, you will have won a victory that you never dreamed of.

Keep firing away with good words at the objective you wish to win, and it will soon be yours. Don't repeat error of any sort—don't even say the words—and finally good words with their subsequent good deeds and results will be the rule instead of the exception in your life. Wonderful discoveries will come to you and with it a great, grand feeling of a kingdom which is whole, a kingdom which is not divided and which will stand.

Let There Be Light

The troop train jogged along at a disgustingly slow gait, stopping at intervals and making long tiresome waits. Night finally came on, and darkness hovered about like a heavy, black mantle. There was a period of quiet. Finally, at the far end of the boxcar, a soldier found a stub of a candle in his kit and lit it. "Oh, light!" was the murmur that went around the crowd, and then a mad scramble ensued to get near it. Some to read, others to sit in it, and others to get a view of it—but one thing for sure—all were seeking it. The light drew all men unto it.

And so is it with the waiting world. They are all hungry for light. They have lived in the dark, damp cave of mortal reasoning long enough and are groping for the sunlight of truth. Darkness and ignorance go hand in hand and with them sin and death. They are of one and the same fabric. In the darkened cloisters of an old cathedral, you will find the faithful praying a prayer of ignorance, a prayer of beseeching and begging instead of realization. "All things are yours" ... "All that the Father has is thine." Come out into the light of understanding and acknowledge that which is already yours—thrill with the joy of gratitude.

No wonder the Master said, "Let there be light." When he said *let*, he did not mean that we were to stay on bended knees for hours, begging for light. "Let" in this sense means "permit or allow." Then he said, "Let your light so shine before men." You have a light all of your own—it is the individuality of you, the you of you—and this light is the light of Love which is filtered through your mind, which is reflected by you, which you let loose through the channel provided.

Let There Be Light

Did you know that you were a "keeper of light?" A keeper not in the sense of hoarding up light—for such a thing were impossible—but a keeper as the keeper of light in the lighthouse tower. You have but to keep your mind open and free from worldly darkness—keep the lenses of your mind polished and shining—to give forth this light so abundantly that all men shall be drawn unto you.

I care not what your business may be. If you bring light into it, you will "draw all men" unto you. You will draw all success and happiness unto it. For the darkened world is searching for a gleam of light and will find you, no matter what your location or how far you may seem removed from the rest of the world. "Ye are the light of the world." The light which is within the tower on the hill cannot be hid—neither can your light be obscured.

Did you know that with that simple yet majestic command, "Let there be light," you have the "open sesame" to all material problems? That all doors are opened before it and no complication of mortal reasoning or doings can withstand the potency of it! When the day is breaking, what a wonderful prayer to say in your heart of hearts: "Let there be light to guide me through this day." What a wonderful day of light would be yours. It would come flooding and streaming in on you as you went your way, until men would recognize you as a "Keeper of Light" and would come to you to seek the light on their problems. "Let there be light" may be just the thing, just the prayer that you need, to break the ice of materialism and free the imprisoned river of your activity.

If your mind is full of light, then no darkness can enter there—no ignorance, sin, or death—for Light and Life are one and are eternal. Let a soft, white, glowing light of truth accompany you, be a part of your speech and a part of your life. Let it enfold you like a mantle "white and glistening." Jesus did this, and those who came within reach of him were healed by the light.

Light shining on the darkness of Earth draws from it the secret of the flowers—draws from the dead, dense mentality the flowers of hope, fruits of use, and trees of strength. So turn your light inward sometimes and let it shine on the darkened corridors of your mind. Make a lighthouse of your darkened chambers—fill them with praise, put on the garments of light.

"Arise, shine; for thy light is come, and the glory of the Lord is risen upon thee." "Let your light so shine before men."

Only, I say, *let*. Be still and let.

"Ye are the light of this world. A light that is set on an hill cannot be hid."

Leaves of the Tree

Failure to Demonstrate

Along the road from sense to soul, the truth seeker meets, from time to time, earnest, sincere pilgrims almost overcome with their burden of failure to demonstrate the principle which they have tried so hard to follow.

They come at you somewhat after this manner: "I have read daily; I have declared the allness of God and that His perfect child cannot be sick, cannot want. I have lived morally and mentally as near the teachings of our revered leader as I know how. I have had treatment from a dozen or more practitioners and have followed their instructions carefully, and yet the demonstration is only partially made or not made at all. What am I to do more?"

These remarks are usually accompanied by signs of the greatest and most absolute faith in the power of God to perform these wonders, and yet if the case is looked into it, might well merit the rebuke of the Master: "O ye of little faith."

In every instance, failure to make manifest the truth which Jesus taught and demonstrated and left for us as an example, with the promise "even greater works than these shall ye do," is directly traceable to lack of faith.

A statement like this is usually received by a vigorous denial on the part of the pilgrim. He is sure he is full of faith. Yet look a little further, and you will see that no sooner does he utter a prayer or apply the principle of Truth than does he begin looking to see if anything is happening. Not satisfied with the efficacy of one prayer, he keeps going over it all day in an almost automatic fashion which, if analyzed, would border on self-hypnosis. It is not the prayer and the truth of it that is holding the preponderance of his thought, but the fear that "nothing is happening," and unconsciously this stimulates him to greater anxiety and causes him to go over and over his petition, entertaining perhaps unconsciously the thought that by repetition he will make clearer just what must happen.

Words are "vain repetition." Bringing this to the attention of the pilgrim, he will answer almost invariably, "We are told to 'pray without ceasing,'" not understanding that the praying without ceasing does not mean a constant repeating of words, but a fixed faith and a contemplation of the reality of man's existence. The unceasing prayer, then, is the thought which, when tempted to repeat and go over work already done, quickly answers the anxiety for a sign with the powerful words: "It is done. I have followed out the Master's instructions. I have knocked, and it shall be opened unto me. I have asked and I shall receive. I have sought and I shall find." God's promises are kept, for "He that promised is faithful."

We are told that "the kingdom of heaven cometh not with observation." Demonstration is like the planting of seeds. They do not grow by constant observation. If you doubt this, try this experiment. Plant two seeds. After planting them, allow one of them to remain untouched and unobserved; the other, dig up twice a day and examine it carefully. Endeavor to find out the exact moment the hard shell cracks which is keeping from you the promise of a flower. Handle it with utmost precaution and examine it under the microscope to detect any possible change.

After a week of this treatment, go back to the untouched seed, and more than likely you will find it has pushed through the hard shell and also through the earth which covered it, while the seed of constant examination has probably shriveled up and died. You do not know the precise moment the change came to the first seed, but the law you made for it when you dropped it into the ground and left it was: "It is done."

Failure to Demonstrate

Unconsciously, when we plant seeds in our gardens, we water them with absolute faith. We leave them with the thought, "I have planted, and eventually I shall reap the harvest of flowers, vegetables, or grain." In the case of the second seed, you planted it with doubt. This was so strong that you constantly dug it up to see if anything was happening, and in your anxiety you wanted to assist it in its working of the problem—you wanted to help it along by observation, and so the promise was not fulfilled.

The treatment which is given with absolute faith will be allowed to accomplish its mission with the same abandon as a planted seed. There will be no constant searching for a sign. Such work will be productive of good results. Perhaps it will be instantaneous and appear at once, as the mushroom appears overnight. Perhaps it will be longer in its unfolding, as the oak tree coming from the acorn. But one thing is sure: it cannot and will not fail to produce after its kind when it is watered with the faith which knows "It is done."

The thought which goes over and over a treatment, though it may call itself faith, is the fear that prayer does not always work, that it is sometimes efficacious and other times not. God will do His work aright without the assistance of mortal mind, and in a way which always mystifies the mortal thought, for His ways are higher than our ways. They are not in any sense our ways.

The writer had a clear and concrete example of this recently. Early in the fall, a dozen or more bulbs were planted in water. Part of the containers were placed in the basement in the dark, and the others were brought up in a heated room of the house in the light. Every day, in passing the bulbs, they were examined. The receptacles were turned a little, the water replenished, and while the bulbs were not exactly handled, they were more or less moved and touched by anxious fingers, and they were under the constant observation of everyone. At the end of six weeks, the house bulbs had attained a height of three inches, while the ones in the basement were standing eighteen inches and were in full bud, ready to bloom.

In the silence, in "the secret place" where the observation of mortal mind is dimmed, is the place to do your work. "The Father within me, he doeth the works." In the secret place, we can declare the allness of God and that His perfect idea, man, is being manifested in its own natural way, which is always beautiful and grand. Then when it is ready for presentation to the world, it will be so evident that it will call itself from the housetops. The perfume of its blossoms will not need attention called to them. They, by their glory and attainment, will attract the notice which is necessary and shall be for an example of faith. "In the twinkling of an eye ... all shall be changed."

Wait on the Lord, "and he shall give thee the desires of thine heart," we are told, and those who "wait upon the Lord ... shall run, and not be weary; and walk, and not faint." Gradually man begins to see that he can of himself do nothing and that the sooner he discontinues his efforts the sooner his demonstration shall be made. The sooner his demonstration shall be made *manifest* is more correct, for the demonstration is already made, always has been made and can never be unmade. It merely awaits being called into manifestation. Man then comes to the conclusion that his chief work is to know how to "wait patiently."

Waiting patiently does not mean procrastination, or putting off. Nor does it mean the fatalistic handling so badly misunderstood: "Well, if it's best for me, I shall have it," for unless this is understood properly, it makes one a mere pawn in the game of chance.

Waiting patiently does mean faith in God—faith that God not only can but will accomplish and has in fact already

Failure to Demonstrate

accomplished our desires and "will bring everything to our remembrance." This kind of faith is the song of glory: "It is done, it is done." When man has found the blessed Truth as revealed to him by the writings of Mary Baker Eddy, he has a right to expect and declare that "Christ has rolled the stone away from the door of human hope" (*Science and Health*). He has a right, a divine right, to expect that his sincere, honest desires shall be made manifest to him here and now, or else his study is in vain.

He who prays after this fashion shall know what is meant by "Let your light so shine before men." He shall know that *let* does not mean *make*. He shall know that the letting is the easiest and most beautiful thing in the world, which will take place as unpretentiously and as gloriously as the coming of dawn. Gradually the flood of light, understanding, and completed demonstration shall steal over him, for the obstacle has been moved from the cave of his limitations, and he steps free, untrammeled.

In looking over the works of our Master, one finds almost the keynote of his work in the expression "I can of mine own self do nothing" but "with God all things are possible." If Jesus, the Wayshower, used this law so perfectly and stated it so well for us, if he acknowledged that he could of himself do nothing, it should open our eyes to the futility of our trying to aid the Divine.

If any man doubt this, let him go into his garden and pick a rosebud and try to make it blossom by use of his mortal fingers. What will be his results but a blasted promise, neither bud nor rose.

Then pilgrim take heart. Send your prayer with the same sweet assurance that you plant a seed, knowing that having done this, you have done all that you can do. Let it go from you with the same freedom that you drop your letters into the post office box, and presently, perhaps before you expect it, the answer will come back, freighted with joy and happiness.

Letting Go

Perhaps one of the most difficult things to the growing student is the ability to let go. He makes a reality of the very things which he wishes to overcome and in doing so hugs them to him with all his strength, when it is only necessary many times to let go, and the thing which has been hurting or hindering his progress will disappear.

In the Bible, the struggle of Jacob with the unnamed thing is a good illustration of how we hold things to us and suffer from them. When Jacob loosed it and let it go, it disappeared and was no more. What this condition was we are not told, but if it was one of sickness or poverty or hatred, it was one and the same thing. The process of being able to let go is one of the most freeing things possible.

In the first place, when a man loosens his hold on a thing, he can then move away from it if the thing does not want to move from him. Some men are carrying around loads so large and out of proportion to their size that they can hardly accomplish the meanest tasks because they are handicapped and because all their energy is used or sapped in holding onto the condition which they want to be rid of.

In Africa, one of the ways of capturing a monkey is by making a small hole in a coconut and filling the coconut with some most edible grain. Presently the monkey puts his hand in the opening and closes it on the handful of grain, thereby increasing the size of his fist to such an extent that he cannot again withdraw his hand from the hole. At this point, the hunter appears, and the frightened monkey, who might scamper off into the jungle to his freedom, tries to drag the coconut after him and is caught. His condition is exactly like the man who has a problem which he is not able to let go of. He does not realize that by relaxing his hold the thing would slip from him and he would be free and able to go where he would.

This is the doctrine of "resist not." When a man resists a thing, it is a pretty sure sign that he fears it. Resisting also produces friction, which wears a man out and makes him worthless. "Resist not" does not in any way mean that a person should let go of their very being and let the wind of chance handle them as it sees fit, but it does mean letting go of the claims which are objectionable to us and also a refusal to acknowledge them as such realities that they need to be fought or resisted. That which we resist is real, and a thing that is real cannot be put from us. If you feel that your present condition is an absolute reality and that it cannot be changed, rest assured that no amount of thinking will change it, for your thought is holding it in place. Until you change your thought, stop resisting the thing, make of it a thing that can be overcome, you will never gain the goal of your dreams.

If you realize that you were given dominion over everything, then why waste your time resisting a thing? Why not come out with your authority and command the situation? But it would not be fair to either you or the thing which you were resisting if you did not give it the same chance to get away as you take to get away from it. Loose it, therefore, and let it go.

Judge not from appearances, but judge righteous judgment. Refuse to accept the testimony of the material sense which is reporting inharmony to you, but pass the powerful thought along to the uttermost part of your kingdom:

I am well and I know it—because the great God
of whom I am an expression (pressed out idea) has

made me well and strong, and I am in rapport with Him.

Meditate upon this. Realize that it is as impossible for you to express an inharmonious condition as it is for God to express one. If you admit for a minute that the great, all-powerful mind of God can express inharmony of any sort, then you have destroyed your premise that God is all good, and your possible escape from the ills of the flesh is small.

When we come to the "resist not" state and understand that we are henceforth not going to fight a thing with all our might and main—and at the same time say it is "nothing but a thought and a wrong one"—we will come to the place that Jesus came to when he began his demonstrations with a perfect acknowledgement of the completed work: "I thank thee, Father, that thou has heard me." He was so clear in regard to the working of the all-powerful Mind that he was able to give thanks for Its enactment before he saw the results. He was so sure that there was a power which could operate on the behalf of mankind, healing and curing all the ills of the flesh, that he never once used long and difficult argument. He knew the power was with him, and he knew that the power is with any man who is clean enough mentally to receive it.

Instantaneous demonstration is only a miracle in the sense that it is something which sets aside a material law, but a miracle is in reality the natural and perfect enactment of the divine or infinite law, and when we learn more how to use this law, we will be able to do the things that Jesus did with the same ease.

"The things that I do, ye shall do also, and even greater." We are not only to do the things he did but even greater. What did he do?

> Raised the dead, opened the blind eyes, unstopped the deaf ears; healed the lame, made well the sick.

Turned water into wine, produced gold from the fish's mouth, made plentiful increase in the place where lack was.

"The things that I do, ye shall do also, and even greater." It is thundering down the ages with a new meaning. Awake thou that sleepest, to the glorious possibilities of your oneness with this illimitable Power, Good. This is your divine heritage. This is your birthright, and it can only be reclaimed by right thinking.

Every condition is in reality a state of consciousness. This may be difficult for you to see at first, but as you go into the workings of the law of right thinking, you will realize that the very place you are now in is the place your thought has put you. But the glorious thing that comes to all people who are alive and thinking is that no matter what place they are in, they can, by proper thinking, change that place to one more to be desired, or else they can change the place where they now are to one which will be amply satisfactory for their every need and happiness.

It is quite true that the kingdom of heaven is right at hand—it is only a matter of how a man looks at it. With the eyes of the right thinking man, he sees God, Life, manifested everywhere, and he becomes one with the great plan of nature and hence is in perfect harmony with the whole scheme. This brings the peace which passeth all understanding—and brings contentment, that most cherished gift of all.

It is not necessary, then, to begin worrying about the material condition about you. First look to the mental state. Get that right, and as you turn to the Father, or the Christ-Consciousness, you will find that the Father, Christ-Consciousness, is turning to you, and you are welcomed back into the land of plenty and happiness.

Suddenly, in the very place which has been the desert existence to you, the rose shall bloom. Infinite possibilities will open unto you, friends will flock to you, for remember, you are now working with the *one* and *only* law that is worthy of consideration, and this law operates "in the twinkling of an eye." Suddenly, as this change comes, you will find yourself ready for it, for the change has been going on within for a long time, and the secret thing has at last been declared from the housetops.

The difficulty experienced by most people in getting results is that they start with the effect instead of the cause. This is because in most instances they recognize the effect as the cause.

If a man is in debt, he constantly meditates upon that debt. He looks at it as a cause instead of an effect. He constantly contemplates it with fear, and nine chances out of ten, he puts into action the law "the thing I feared has come upon me." That is done by "the law of attraction." Remember that like attracts like, and if you want certain conditions to manifest in your life, you can never attain them as long as you keep your mind full of the opposite views of life.

All about you, you can see instances where the law of attraction has been working. The average man who is down and out in the world is always talking hard times, failure. He is fault-finding and pessimistic. He believes in the will-o-the-wisp chance, and he attracts all these conditions to him permanently because like attracts like.

Look at the lives of big men. Some of them have failed many times, but they "never say die." One failure teaches them the lesson they needed, and they go at it again with the feeling "Well, I made it once, I can do it again." That is what prompts them on, and they usually arrive.

Like physical exercise, the repeated, systematic exercise will surely result in enlarged muscles, increased strength and vitality, and so with mental gymnastics. If you are faithful to your period of silent communion with the All-Power and realize your oneness with It, you will begin to see increased mental powers, and finally when you take a check on life, you will find you have made tremendous strides towards your goal. "I have done that once, I can do it again" is the encouragement which you pass along to your success, little though it may be. And when a thing is well repeated, the person is ready to go higher.

The old threadbare axiom "Practice makes perfect" we all recognize. I remember passing a certain residence the very day the young daughter had her first lesson on the piano. The thought came to me, "What a far reach it is to a place where she will be able to interpret Chopin correctly." Yet when I passed that way daily, I could begin to detect improvement almost from the start, and one day she was playing the preludes of the master with great ease. I could well remember when she did not know one note from the other, and to have placed a prelude in front of her then and say, "Play that" would have been utterly foolish on the face of it. Yet you realized at that time that the child had the ability to do it if she were only willing and ready to set out on the faithful path of a little consistent study each day.

Perhaps you stand today where the little girl at the piano was that first day. Are you willing to take up a little sincere and careful thinking for a few moments a day in order to come into the possession of your dreams?

We soon learn that if we would have control of the outer man we must first get control of the inner. We must begin to realize that the outer is only a manifestation of the inner and that in proportion as we wish to change a

Letting Go

thing, we must first seek the cause of that condition or thing within.

Once you have decided to eliminate a certain condition from your life, from that moment on never give voice to the lie again. When it presents itself to you, dismiss it with the abiding conviction that it is a lie and has no place in your mind or body. Make your strong affirmations and cling to them. Once you have learned that the inner source is capable of anything, you will hold before it only such patterns as you wish reproduced. But if you have already reproduced something that is objectionable, you can yet return to the "secret place" and there destroy the thought which created it in the first place. Remember to look only to the cause; the effect will take care of itself.

Having decided that you will rid yourself of some claim, you must learn to meditate upon the state or condition which you wish to replace it with. Idealize it, praise it, and know that you have dropped the seed into fertile ground and that it is springing into birth.

Keep silent about your shortcomings, your faults, your fears, and sickness. The more you repeat them the more real they become to both yourself and others, and voicing these errors only accentuates their reality.

Eliminate weak words from your mind and your vocabulary. See how often you can substitute a powerful word for one of limitation and weakness. How often do we hear the expressions "I was scared nearly to death," "tickled to death," "I nearly died laughing," etc., all of which have their effect on the body and mind of man. They are weak, wasteful words which could and should be replaced with words of beauty and life.

After a little while of this watchfulness, you will find it becoming a habit—the habit of speaking only good, strong words and of thinking this kind of thoughts. You will then enter into a perpetual state of happiness, for you will be free from the limitations that your false words have fixed upon you.

Cast Your Bread upon the Waters

In most people's thought, the word *cast* means to fling away, to let go of with the thought of no return, but in the parable under consideration, the word has quite a different meaning.

In the first place, the expression came into use by reason of the rice planter. He was casting his bread upon the water, and it always returned in many days, increased.

This is a much more fruitful interpretation to consider than merely throwing a crust of bread upon the waters to be washed into the port of some needy one. It carries with it the idea of progress. When we give, we plant. When we cast the word of truth from us, we literally plant the seed of truth, and in many days we again see the "bread" increased, returning to us.

This is particularly true of work done for others. It springs into full fruitage, and we again are refreshed by a return of the word. For we only keep that which we give. The thing which is unused falls apart or rusts. Of nothing is this more true than the unused talent which we hold in the innermost part of our being. If we conceal it from others and withhold it, in times of great trouble, when we seek it, we find that it has vanished. The seed of anything cannot be kept indefinitely. If it is not planted or cast upon the waters, sooner or later the life (spirit or inspiration) of it dies, and we have nothing but the material form (the letter).

Now, the letter without the Spirit is dead, and so is the seed without the life germ. Confidently does the planter scatter his rice upon the waters. It disappears immediately from sight. Does he become fearful that it will all be consumed by fishes and insects? Does he immediately after planting go for a net and try to regain that which he has cast away? No. As he plants, he also knows that the increase is already his, and this increase comes by reason of his ability to let go of the seed.

Do you know that you cannot cast a word of truth from you that is not productive of good results, though it may not be immediately visible to you? Do not be afraid to speak the truth whenever you see the water is waiting for the seed. It will return unto you with the increase in many days.

God

That which underlies, overlies, and encompasses all true being, that which permeates infinity, that which constitutes all force and energy—that is God, Principle.

God, the infinite, omnipotent, omniscient, omnipresent force of the universe is the one and only cause of all that is.

God, the great and universal law of everything, is expressed through His idea, man, bringing into view His wonderful attributes, such as love, purity, truth, health.

Everywhere we look, we find God, from the chirping of the cricket to the "music of the spheres," from the energy of the most minute insect to the tremendous force of the mighty river. "Whether we look, or whether we listen, we hear life murmur, or see it glisten" (James Russell Lowell)—a whole universe full of throbbing, vibrant life, charging the least atom of being with its magnificent energy and power; endowing us with its super strength and placing in our hands the scepter of dominion. "I have not given thee the spirit of fear, but of power and a strong mind." Such is Life, the vitalizing substance of God, which flows to us constantly, regenerating and rejuvenating us and making us anew.

The attributes of God are brought from the abstract into the concrete through the medium of man. Here we see man inspired with generosity and kindness. He goes far into the bypaths of life, doing good and on missions of Love. Gradually he takes on the Christlike quality of compassion, and we understand what is meant by the abstraction *compassion*, and so on through the category of his attributes.

The bringing forth of these attributes enriches the nature of man, enlarging his vision and pushing out the "borders of his tent" until the practical demonstration of all his attributes is made manifest and man reaches the perfection of which he now but dreams.

God is health, and since "in him we live and move and have our being," we are literally in a sea of perfect strength. We have but to let go of our limited sense of health to bring into manifestation the universal law of perfect health. We cease to speak of "my" health and think no more of it than we do of the great envelope of air that enfolds us. We simply draw on this vast never-ending and inexhaustible infinity of health and life, and it is ours. When we learn to dismiss the personal idea of health, a permanent demonstration of health is made. Man can then be truly "absent from the body and present with the Lord."

As man becomes conscious that he is an instrument upon which breathes the divine impetus, or energy, he gives himself over to the Master for the work which will best express Him. His talent, which has long been buried under the debris of material wonder, worry, and reasoning, is now uncovered and brought to light, inflated, as it were, with the divine breath, energy, and turned to some good account. As he pushes this talent to its limits, the Master of the garden returns, and finding him a faithful servant, he adds the ten talents and the power to bring them into manifestation.

As man drops the limited personal idea of supply, he gains the unlimited substance of mind, and he ceases to speak of "my dollars and land." He uses that which he needs and that which comes into his hands as legitimate supply. It is in making the connection with the inexhaustible source of substance that man demonstrates his needs.

Since all good things come of God, desire is born of Him. Insofar as desire is good, it is, so to speak, the thing in its incipiency, which is pressing towards man for expression. Once man is properly contacted with God, the infinite Cause of all, he becomes a channel for all good,

God

and his desires run and disport themselves into the flesh—that is, they materialize.

A knowledge of God as first and only Cause lifts man above and beyond all manmade laws, all universal beliefs and fears which the flesh is heir to. That which has heretofore been considered with a certain amount of reverence inspired by fear is immediately uncovered and made void.

Recently a case of fear and failure came to my attention through the so-called law of the planets. The person in question had had a horoscope cast at an extremely large fee and by a so-called master, but when it arrived it was so pernicious, and I might say vicious, in its treatment of this life that the poor subject to whom it belonged was of all people most desolate. There was not a single redeeming feature in the whole thing. And all this was heaped upon a poor individual because, without consent or knowledge, he had been born upon a certain day.

A fear took possession, followed by depression and gloom, when the case came to my attention. All the bright hopes and ambitions were suddenly dashed into the dust, and an aching void stood before and stretched out over weary years. Then it was that the asking of a simple question put to flight this nightmare and forever broke the self-mesmeric state of horoscopic law. "Who came first, God or the planets?" And since God is all-power and all-present, what need or reason would He have for assigning to a group of stars power to annihilate one of His children? If God is all-power and all-present, why should you fear such a so-called thing as influence of the planets, which are millions of miles away and derive all their power from God?

And so through the application of God as First Cause, man can destroy with scientific certainty all fear of unknown influences and forces, and likewise heredity, prenatal influences and pre-dispositions, eccentricities, and faith in mediums, diviners, and wizards. They stand powerless and, I might add, senseless before this one and only primal and ever-lasting Cause, God.

When we seek Him in the temple of our bodies, we find him knocking at the door of our sin-bound hearts. There in the darkness of material fears, failures, and worries, He awaits us, ready to sup with us in perfect contentment and to place in our hands the scepter of dominion. And gradually we come upon the sacred word *Father*, which is breathed from the inmost recesses of our soul with the velvet lips of silence. What a glorious, swelling paean of praise breaks forth, as though it would burst the delicate heart. Like the vigorous mountain stream, tearing and dashing through the ravine carrying tons of refuse and debris before it without a conscious effort, so this soul-stirring word, *Father*, when spiritually discerned, crashes through time-honored material conditions and customs, washing everything clean with the River of Life.

Presently we find the body a "well watered garden" by the banks of the ever-flowing River of Life, and we find it an exceedingly pleasant and comfortable place to dwell in. As we learn to live in this River of Life, to direct its course upward instead of downward, we come to a fine, almost mystic thing, a power which, though mental and spiritual, is almost visible. It goes whither it will, regardless of material conditions, and accomplishes wonders by merely resting upon an object. It sweeps away the dirty web of material reasoning in which man has been ensnared so long. It takes issue with disease and heals without an effort because it is conscious only of perfection. It transforms that which is torn down and mutilated and looses the chains of the captives of sense.

Presently man learns that the Garden so well-watered and cared for is also a temple of the living God, a place wherein he may retire from the worldly strife and stir and commune consciously with "Father." He soon learns that in time of trouble he can hide in the tabernacle of his God; that he can enter suddenly into the counsel chamber of his God and ask advice and guidance; that he can carry his load of gratitude to God and "bear a song away."

After he learns the word *Father* in its spiritual sense and meaning, he comes upon a new word, and that is *brother*, a word which he carries from the inner sanctuary out into the world as a sweet incense and anointing oil of love to pour upon the broken hearts. And as he ministers along the wayside of life, presently the Father speaks and says, "Inasmuch as ye have done it unto the least of these, ye have done it unto me."

What more shall we say of such a radiant Love, which enfolds us with a tender mother affection, which soothes and forgives and offers us anew His gifts in super-abundance.

As a Man Thinketh

"As a man thinketh in his heart, so is he." On every hand, we hear a great deal about the control of mind over matter. In fact, we have always heard of it, but a large majority of us have passed it by with the comment "will power," "not lasting," "theory," etc.

First, does the thought affect the body? Take, for example, the boy who wants to go swimming and has been told no. What is the expression of his face? And if he has work to perform, notice how he moves with the action of an aged man. Say to this boy, "You can go." It is like touching an electric button. Life literally shoots through him. He jumps, throws his hat in the air, smiles until it is positively contagious, and then runs off, happy as a lark. Did thought have anything to do with changing a lagging, fatigued body into a powerful little machine that operated at a tremendous high rate of speed? Think about this. It is by these simple steps that we are going to build up to things worthwhile and that will accomplish.

Bring a message of death into a happy family, and watch the rapid change. They have seen nothing. Actually they know nothing for a fact except what the paper says. Tears start, souls are wrung, agony comes over all, and the cheery, happy home is made unhappy in the twinkling of an eye. By what? A change in thought.

Suppose, after seeing this grief displayed, that the message proves to be a mistake. In an instant, the family is rushed back into joy and happiness. "All shall be changed in the twinkling of an eye"—by thought. I ask you: what has become of the sorrow? I ask you: where did it come from and where did it go? Think on these things; they are steps to the temple of thought we are building.

How many of us have not seen a violent headache follow a great spell of anger or hatred? No blows were struck, and yet the person by his thought caused himself to have a headache. You have also read or heard of cases where people fell dead in a fit of anger. Apoplexy from anger is not an uncommon thing, even recorded in medical journals. There are many kinds of thought, but suppose we take that of fear for a moment and look into it.

As a child, you probably copied into your writing books this old adage: "Cowards die many times before their death." We have all heard of death which has been caused by fear. It is the taskmaster of the age. It is the thing that stalks about in darkness and makes slaves of us. It is the thing that keeps us under and in bondage, either to sickness, poverty, or public opinion, but it is glorious news to tell you that when you examine into fear you find it is made of the same substance as the ghost of childhood. It is nothing but a state of thought. Where does the child's fear go when you bring a light? Yet men go on fearing and teaching the child to be afraid.

You have often read the old fable of the Plague going to Baghdad to kill five thousand people. Later when met, he was accused not of killing five but fifty thousand. "No" said the Plague, "I killed only five thousand—fear killed the rest."

So now we come to the conclusion that the greatest gift which God has given man is the power to think. We begin to realize that to think, we must have thoughts, and we begin to see that the state of body, thus far at least, is affected by the kind of thoughts we think.

We shall liken ourselves to a very fine and sensitive plate which records everything with which it comes in contact. What would be the natural instinct if you had such a plate? Would you not want to protect it from meeting disagreeable things and shelter it from disagreeable subjects? I think so. So we find that the very first and perhaps one of the simplest tasks to begin with is to place a guard at the entrance of the temple, that nothing which "defileth … or maketh a lie" can enter. In plain English: we will begin to watch our thoughts and not give our time to rash thinking along lines which are sure to produce evil results.

Invisible Power

In entering upon a critical study of a subject so vast as our mental heritage, perhaps the first stumbling block which everyone encounters is: how can an unseen, unfelt, almost unknown "something," which is abstract in every sense of the word, be applied to affect my everyday material life?

The doubt that this is a present possibility is the very thing which holds many from the study of the most exact, and at the same time most remunerative, of sciences in life; in fact we might add, keeps them from investigating and applying the one science which, in applying properly, would enable them to understand and operate all other sciences with greater ease and intelligence than could possibly be gained from approaching the subject from the other end.

At the beginning of our journey into that vast and wonderful country of desire, we are first confronted with doubt. Jesus, the greatest healer the world has ever known, said in plain language that all about us was a great, undeveloped thing called the kingdom of heaven—that is, that all about us lay the very things we most desired, yet we, having eyes, see not, and ears, we hear not, because the material sense at once demands that we handle the kingdom of heaven with our material hands and thrust our hands into the wound of material workings before we can accept a thing. We are, as I have said, at the very beginning of our journey beset with the most dreaded of mental obstacles—doubt.

Like Thomas, a great many of us stand ready to believe, if we only can "thrust our hands into the wound" and make sure that it is identically the same wound that a material sword or spear has made. If we have this proof at

A Royal Diadem *and* Leaves of the Tree

the beginning, we are willing to go ahead gaily, for there are few people today who do not realize, in some measure at least, that there must be a cause, a primal cause, for all our longing and desires.

We, as a race, have come to the place where we ask ourselves over and over, "Why do I have such desires with no seeming possibility of fulfillment? From where did these desires originate? And gradually individuals are emerging from the struggling mass of humanity and entering into the kingdom of heaven on earth. They do not necessarily change their place of residence; they are not suddenly borne off on wings or carried out of sight. No, the kingdom of your desires is not a locality—it is simply a state of your mind. Again, to quote the master metaphysician: Look not "lo here, or lo there," for the kingdom of heaven is at hand; it is within you.

But how to get there, how to come within sight of our kingdom of heaven, might be put in a more simple way: How am I to rid myself of this colossal doubt which assails me, when I cannot see, feel, hear, touch, smell this wonderful thing towards which I am journeying or striving to journey?

Someone has said, "Reason is the most active human faculty." The master metaphysician admonished, "Come, let us reason together." Let us then reason a little on the subject of the invisible power which is to change our lives.

When we stop to consider for a single moment our existence, we find that without a question of a doubt our whole lives are guided by something that we cannot see. Take the municipal law, for instance. Did you ever see it? Did you ever smell it? Did you ever taste it, hear it? No, you never did. In reality, there is nothing tangible about it. You cannot in any way contact it with anything material, yet you know that in your very community it exists all the time, that it is active and that you are protected by it. You are not afraid that the average man in the street is going to snatch your purse, is going to kill you, is going to break into your house, and yet neither you nor he can see anything called municipal law. Yet it is there and operates all the same.

"Ignorance of the law excuses no man." If a man breaks the law, though he plead ignorance he must still pay the penalty. If he kills a man and thinks in his ignorance he has a right to, he must soon feel the invisible thing close in around him like a net and exact the utmost farthing from him.

If this be true of the material workings of a man's life, it is much more true of the mental side of his existence. If he pays the penalty for a broken material law, he will also pay the penalty for a broken mental or spiritual law, and every day we have ample proof of the lawbreakers all about us. This man is sick, this man is unhappy, this man is poor, this man is friendless—all these conditions are the direct result of broken mental laws. When we come to realize this and face the matter squarely, we will know that our ignorance of the law was not excused, that we have paid dearly for it, and we will set ourselves about learning the proper application of the most vital force in the universe.

Reversing the generally accepted idea of the workings of the mind, we find that it is simplicity itself. Once we have gained the victory over doubt, we find that we stand at the foot of a wondrous flight of steps, each one a distinct gain and growth leading to final victory over the so-called laws of material life, at length placing us in the midst of the kingdom of heaven—right here and now. We suddenly apprise ourselves of the startling knowledge that we do not have to die to get into heaven, but that by proper living and thinking, we can live ourselves into it right here and now.

There are many in the world today who are fast approaching the walls of "the city four square," which is the city beautiful of their every desire, and you too can win this goal if you are willing to devote a little time each day to proper thinking and a proper application of thought to your daily life.

Let us not be too anxious. Let us not be too observing of our progress, but rather, keep our eyes fixed on the goal and not on the road leading to it, and presently, while we are still busily engaged with working out our salvation, we come within sight of the city of our dreams.

Think on These Things

"Now are we the sons of God ... we know that when he shall appear (be made manifest to us in the flesh), we shall be like him, for we shall see (understand) him as he is."

The time for the awakening of man to his divine heritage is at hand.

God is Mind. God is Life. If God is the only life of man, then all there is to man that really matters is God. Life is all there is to you. When you cease to think, you cease to live, and when you cease to live, you cease to have a consciousness of God.

What we know as Man, in the highest sense of the word, is merely God made conscious.

Think of this for a moment. God is the infinitude of Mind. Think of a limitless Mind. Now then, certain ideas begin to come to the surface of this Mind and become conscious. If we can imagine a speck in Mind, and this speck being conscious, then we can get the idea of the Man of the God-man which is an individual expression, though joined to the parent Mind, as the branch is one with the tree.

If God is the only life of man, then all there is to you is God. You are simply the means of God being expressed in His highest form. God without man would be a nonentity—that is, if these points of consciousness, or expressions, were to be taken away, then God would simply be the great vast Mind unexpressed.

If your life is God, then look into the nature of God and find out what is *your* precise nature.

Suddenly, when you become conscious that your very own life is God, you are awake in a way you have never dreamed of being before. You realize that you have dominion, for you are no more asking the body or material conditions the what and wherefore of life, but you take the reins in hand and control the whole thing. You are suddenly the man in authority, and this awakening will so open your eyes to the great healing possibilities of this consciousness that you will immediately begin the work of instantaneous healings.

"Awake, awake, thou that sleepest (those that imagine there is a man-idea separate from God), and Christ shall give thee light." You shall awake with the brightness of His coming, for He is surely coming, and when you just hark back to the idea that *my Life is God*, then you begin to realize that He is very close, "closer than breathing, nearer than hands and feet," because God is all there is. God is infinite.

You are simply one expression of an infinite Mind—individual and progressive but never separate, never subservient to matter, never at a loss to know what to do, but always speaking with authority and power.

The Lord is Mindful of His Own

Fear not—the Lord will supply your every need. Only believe. When the people needed bread, it appeared each morn and covered the ground. Then they called it manna; today we call it mushrooms. God has infinite ways to accomplish His works, and not one of them is weird or mysterious. They are pleasantly natural.

Fear not. He has guaranteed a safe passage through the storms and through the fire. His refreshing thoughts are today found gushing from every page of the holy book. Come ye and drink. This is the draught of Life and will give thee eternal life.

When the oil ran low and there was nothing left in the house, the Lord supplied joy, and the oil started flowing again. Remember that the cruse of oil is ever full as long as the heart is full of joy. But doubt and grief thicken the oil, and it cannot run.

There are many gifts. To one he gave one thing, to another something else. You shall look within and find out what your gift is and use it for your growth.

Did you know that we are all prophets? We can all prophesy good in the absolute. There is never a sick one who comes to you for help that cannot receive the joy of your prophecy. As you develop this constant prophesying of good, it shall become a power to you, so wonderful and strong that you shall at last be able to not only prophesy but shall be able to "bring it to pass." You shall then raise the gift of prophecy to demonstration.

Begin prophesying today—start right now with any untoward condition that is about you and prophesy its complete correction. Every time you see it, repeat your prophecy, and one day it will come true.

Do you know that ships that pass in the night and signal each other in passing sometimes anchor at the same port? So live, then, that those who pass you on life's highway, on seeing your signal of good cheer, will desire above all things to anchor near you. The vision you hold before you is the thing you will eventually become. As you grow, your signal will reach farther and farther until it shall encircle the entire globe. Today the spoken word is heard around the entire globe; tomorrow the thought back of the word will penetrate infinite space and find its level.

Your signal tower is also a station which receives messages for which it is attuned. You are the sole judge whether these shall be songs of joy or hecatombs of tragedies. You alone are the arbiter of your fate and shall glean from the great world that which you most desire. The world shall be your textbook, and in it you shall find the truth.

Make Love the underlying melody of every message you send out, and love will come back to you. Be sure that while you are looking for that which is not true that you do not miss the truth itself. Nothing is so mean or despicable that it does not contain some grain of good, and there is nothing that lives and breathes that does not respond to the gentle touch of love.

What a message, then, to flash to the world each morning: "God's in His heaven—All's right with the world!"

Your Problem

I know not what your individual problem may be, but just the same, I bring you the glorious message that you can change your present condition. *You can* change sickness to health; *you can* change poverty into wealth; *you can* be that which you desire to be. Further, I say to you that the castle of your dreams *can be attained* here and now by simply gathering up the loose ends of your power and centralizing your energy and force.

Of course, there are different kinds of thinking, and so there are different stages, degrees, and kinds of life. When a man stops thinking, he is dead. Is this not so? Even a lunatic thinks, though he scatters his thought over a great field, taking on the thought of everything that passes by.

Many people scatter thought and are in a constant state of confusion. Such people are like the chameleon placed on a highly colored oriental rug. He changes so rapidly that he represents no one color but is in a constant state of change—nothing definite in the way of color.

The subject we are going to take up is so simple that it seems difficult, but since you are a seeker of light, let us examine into it with unprejudiced mind, try it and see if it is not the truth.

Everybody realizes thought is the dynamic force of the universe. Without thought, where would we be? Take your own home, for instance. What would happen if thought properly directed were not in use?

Do you believe in thought and its effect on your life and body? Go into a church where it is quiet and see if the quiet thought of reverence does not immediately take possession of you. Go into a theater where thousands of people are laughing and cheering and try to weep. Go into an orphan's home and look into the wistful eyes of half a dozen children and try to keep the love thought out of your mind. Go into a penitentiary and see the long lines of men marching to and fro and then try to keep the thought of compassion down.

Your whole life is made up of thought—what you think is what you are.

"As a man thinketh in his heart, so is he" has been quoted over and over, and the truth of it finally dawns on everyone who is really thinking. Our lives are exactly what we think them to be, our position exactly what our thought has made it, our health exactly what we have held in mind regarding our bodies and other people's bodies.

"Nothing is either good or bad but thinking makes it so" might well be rendered: there is nothing *either* good or bad that is not made by thinking.

There is no limit to what you can do when you get hold of the idea of right thinking. There are no walls which will not crumble before the right understanding of the power of thought. There is no mountain which will not be removed and cast into the uttermost parts of the sea if you handle your thought correctly. Again I repeat that the process of thinking rightly is so simple that it seems difficult.

Everybody is seeking the kingdom of heaven. Some of us are looking one place and some another, but all, even the grossest materialist, is seeking this state of happiness which he thinks of in terms of heaven. The great mistake which has always been made, and is largely made today, is that we seek this kingdom in some locality, generally quite remote to our present place, instead of seeking it in the only possible place it can be found—*within you*. Now heed this: the kingdom of your desires fulfilled lies *within you*.

Your Problem

The world or heaven within is lying there, awaiting the coming of the master. You are the master, and we are going to go hand in hand into the kingdom of your most cherished desire and find there that which will make you happy, healthy, prosperous.

Keep in mind that there is no mystery to this work, no hard concentration, no strained positions to be held, or forced thoughts, but a natural unfolding as beautifully easy as the unfolding of a rose in June.

That which you see about you, after all, is the result of that which was at one time hidden in the inner world. Like the seed which was dropped into the earth, when it burst through the darkness, or the invisible, it came out into the objective world and was seen, so with these wonderful flowers of your desire. When they receive the touch of Life which your thinking is presently going to give them, you will soon see them blooming everywhere. For as we have already said, thought is life. Up to this time, the kingdom of your life has been full of seeds, but no urge or life was felt in them, so they remained in the darkness of the invisible.

The secret of live thinking is what we are going to learn. All about you is the great mind of God, the Mind out of which all things were brought forth and from which all things will eventually be brought forth, for it is the formless substance of things hoped for. Now, thought is the creative force which acts on this formless substance and shapes it into that which it desires. Thought makes the mold into which this substance is poured before it is made manifest in the flesh.

Before an architect can build a house, he first conceives it in his mind as complete and perfect. He works out the details of every little part, and then he sets it down on paper. As he does this, he keeps on reaching further, until the mental mold that he made and filled full of the formless substance of mind finally becomes the picture which he first held in mind.

There is nothing unnatural about this. Take it in your own life, for instance. What do you do? Are you a businessman or woman? Do you want to write a letter? Whether you know it or not, you have the picture of it formulated in your mind. Then you go to work, and finally the thing which was just a thought in the beginning becomes a piece of paper with a message written on it. You made the mold and poured it, and finally you have the result. Perhaps you are a housewife, and instead of a letter, you think of a pie. Perhaps you are a minister and you think of a sermon, but no matter what line you follow, no matter what your station in life, the law works just the same.

That is reasonable, you say, and the next step is too. When we come to the point that we can recognize that thought is the creator, then we come to the matter of quality. What is the quality of your thinking?

Perhaps you say, "Well, I never did think of this sickness and I have it" or, "I never did think of this poverty and I have it."

Let me recall to your mind the story of the cobbler who sat working at his little bench, when a camel looked in at the window. The cobbler worked on, and so the camel put his nose in. Not receiving any resistance, he pushed his head in, then his neck, then his hump, and then his whole body sprawled into the room and crowded the cobbler into the corner so tightly that he could not do his work.

"How did you get here? I never invited you in." And when he looked at the small, open window, he almost knew it was impossible for such a large animal to get through such a small opening. But since the camel stood against the closed door, it was impossible for him to get out any other way than the way he had come in, so then the work began in earnest.

Thought is something that needs attention. We must watch it and see that the quality is right. If we want camels of sickness, unhappiness, and poverty to crowd us out of our birthright, then all we have to do is to leave the window open and unguarded, and presently we will be crowded over into the narrow corner of our already too narrow existence. All the light will be shut off, and the air will become foul with these hateful animals which have crept in at unguarded moments.

Now, the matter of guarding your thought need not alarm you. It is not nearly so stupendous a job as it looks. It is merely refusing to accept the destructive thoughts that come to us.

We have got to learn now to judge not from appearances, but to judge righteous judgment. No matter what the seeming conditions of a thing may be, we have enlisted in the army of right-thinking people, and we are going to change the face of the thing and see the new, fine thought manifested right before our eyes.

Mind is like a great storage plant with millions of volts of static electricity waiting for an outlet. Thought is the dynamic force which connects up with this great storage house, and the result is seen in what we create or what the thought pattern was that was taken to the powerhouse. Now, Mind is always and eternally good, and when It is applied properly will accomplish undreamed of wonders, but we must not attempt to use this great force wrongly and expect good results. If an electric wire is left to lie on the ground and a child steps on it and is killed, you could not say that electricity was bad, for you know that same force that seemed to do the damage to the child could have been applied to carry a message thousands of miles or could have run a streetcar or a thousand and one other things. Look, then, to the quality of your thinking.

I do not have to bring to your mind the various proofs of the power of thought. All of us have experiences—some of the optical illusions and the sense illusions which are so common they hardly need mentioning. What boy who has joined a secret order or fraternity has not been burned with an ice-cold poker or felt himself bleeding to death by a small stream of lukewarm water being poured over his arm? Inversely, we all know of instances where thought has carried people far into the most difficult feats. Mothers have been able to do remarkable things for their children in time of peril. Men in battle have been swept on to victory. Everything is the result of thought.

Thought is all there is to existence, so now let us begin with an eliminating process. If we want wealth, we are going to begin to eliminate the poverty idea. If we want health, we are going to begin to eliminate the sick thought. If we want happiness, we are going to eliminate the unhappy thought. How shall we do this?

Listen: all that you desire, the kingdom of heaven, lies within. Then the way to get what we want is to go within and bring it out.

"Not so easy," you say?

"Perfectly easy," I reply to you. "Line upon line, precept upon precept."

Today we are going to begin the journey back into the kingdom and go just as fast as we can find the way.

Let us take an easy position, somewhere in a place as quiet as is possible, and then relax. Relax and let the chair hold you up and get perfectly easy physically. Now close your eyes and rest for a moment. Think of yourself not as a body, not as a person, but as the same carefree individual you are when you dream at night.

Remember how easy it is for you to pass from one place to another in your dream. That is because you don't have to bother with the material body and a lot of other paraphernalia, which we do when waking. Now then, you can take this individuality into the innermost recesses of your mind by declaring, "I am one with the Father within." This was what Jesus did. He knew that the Father within was right thinking, which enabled him to enter the kingdom of heaven. If you are one with the Father within, you are one with goodness, with happiness, with health, with wealth.

You are one with the great Powerhouse in which is stored infinite power to accomplish that which you wish right here and now, and the way is not difficult and hard to find.

Oneness

Mind is infinite, and you are a point in that Mind where it becomes conscious. You are not at any moment disconnected from this parent Mind, but as the islands are one with the Earth and are merely an expression of the Earth, or a portion of it drawn out into visibility from the complete sphere, so are you joined to the infinite Mind. You, then, are merely an expression, or rather, an expresser of this inexhaustible Mind, from which you can immediately draw all that you can possibly desire.

When you begin to realize your oneness with this Mind, you begin to see that all these false claims which have bound you for so long must fall away and that you are free, for you are Spirit and expressing yourself through a body, and not a body inhabited by an unseen thing called Spirit.

You begin to realize that your great power lies in the fact that the *you* of you is Spirit, one in essence with the great mind of God, and that you can now come into your dominion by making the connection between yourself and your Father within.

The more you realize that you are one with the Father within the more harmony, happiness, and contentment will be manifested in your life; the more you will be able to tread upon the little troubles of daily life and surmount the obstacles which confront every traveler in the journey from sense to soul.

Thousands have gone before you and have gained the mastery, and it is also within your ken to do the same thing. There is nothing you cannot overcome by this simple step, and as we go along, we will find it becoming more simple all the while to become one with the Father within.

Oneness

Jesus was the greatest metaphysician that ever lived, and he gave us a complete and perfect set of laws by which to demonstrate the harmony of being, which he explained to us was the natural state of man.

The reason we are striving for this mastership is because we are told it is ours and that we can attain it. We are to become dominant and forceful and be in authority, overcoming all the false and mistaken results of past thinking. "The works that I do, you shall do also, and even greater." This was promised by the Master, and if we do the Master's work and even greater, we too shall become masters. First of all, we want to learn the mastery over thinking. To think correctly is not a difficult process, but it requires a little daily watching and a little daily practice.

The goal, then, before us is that of mastership. This means complete dominion and authority over everything which presents itself to us and which would spoil our sense of harmony. In attaining this, it is good to know that no willful force or willpower is necessary, for that sort of control or mastership is temporal and soon reacts on the person, reducing him to a pitiful state.

Into the hands of the master has been placed *the word*. The word is the vesture of thought and is there for the thought made audible. By the correction of words, we can correct our thoughts as well as vice versa. By arresting evil, critical, revengeful words, we arrest the thought, condemn it to destruction, and so rid ourselves of it before it has time to manifest itself. Suppose an evil word is spoken, how far-reaching do you think it may be? One single word has been known to end in the murder of a man. Do you think that words are not powerful?

In the same way, one single word has saved a man. "Death and life are in the power of the tongue" (Prov. 18:21). Consider well your words. Watch for a whole day and see how many words you can eliminate from your conversation that are weak. *I am* are two words that we use thousands of times a day, and they are also the name of God. "I AM THAT I AM has sent you." If you say, "I am weak," you are connecting up with a great storage plant and letting your wires lie on the ground. Disaster is bound to happen, for the word is powerful and "sharper than a two-edged sword."

"I am poor." No wonder you are poor, with your great feed-wire cast down to the ground and wasting millions of volts of energy and power, all for nothing. Your words, then, will determine the timbre of your thought, and the results of the words are pretty sure to be after the pattern held in mind.

Just for a little practice, sit quietly down and say to yourself, "*I am master of my destiny.*" Repeat it five times, slowly and thinkingly, and see what a fine feeling it gives you. Why? Because it has started the currents of this great Powerhouse on a constructive mission.

There is magic in words. Take the words *I can* and *I can't* and see what mental attitude accompanies them. Look about you for one of your friends who is making free use of *I can't*, and you will see not only a weak mentality but likewise a weak body which is more than likely encountering endless obstacles and more than likely assuming the role of a martyr.

Look again at the *I can* friend, and nine chances to ten there will be a smile on his face, a bright twinkle in his eye, and when it storms within your kingdom, you feel like running posthaste to him and listening to the dominant ring of *I can*. What a song, what a thrill, what a joy to hear it: "I can do that ... I can do that." Try it for a few times, then come along a little further: "*I can be what I desire to be.*" How's that? Fine, isn't it? It gives you the thrill of real living.

Remember that words voiced of others usually find lodgment in our own lives, and before we know it, the camel, which is just an embryonic thought in the beginning, has pushed us into the corner again.

Don't criticize. God has relieved you of the unpleasant duty of passing judgment. "Judge not," for the law is absolute; the judgment you render to another is surely that which will be rendered unto you, only it will be pressed down and running over.

For a week, watch every negative word and eliminate it. See what a vast number of times you have had to withhold your speech, but see if at the end of the week you have not gained something. "She is so hateful; he is so dishonest." Unless you knew what hateful thoughts and dishonest thoughts were, you would never be able to pin them on another. "Yes, I know, but he actually steals. Is it going to help you or him to tell the world about it? No, it is going to add one more grain to your discomfort.

Your word "shall not return unto you void but shall accomplish whereunto it is sent." What kind of words are you going to send out?

The power of the word has been tried many times, in sport. Two or three have decided to greet a perfectly well person with this speech: "How bad you look this morning; you must be feeling bad," and the result produced was sickness. In some of the heathen islands, people are prayed to death as effectively as if they were given slow poison. Unless we get hold of the power of right thinking, we are subject to all these wandering thoughts of which the world is full, and unless we reject them, they enter. To return to our illustration of the camel: we are crowded into the corner, not knowing why.

"Speak as one having authority." *Speak*—the word again is brought into play. Do not be afraid to speak your heart's most cherished desire into the infinite Mind, into the formless substance, and know that it will manifest itself in the desired result. "Speak the word only," and it shall be done.

When you sit in the silence and go within, you can speak the word. You can speak the desire of your heart, knowing that your word shall not return unto you void, but shall accomplish. Then as you hold yourself from weak, vacillating words and thoughts, you will see the seed word germinate and the idea push up into visibility, for words are seeds, and we reap what we sow.

Sow a crop of sick words, and the harvest will be sickness. Sow a crop of health words, and the crop will be strength and power. Some seeds germinate instantly and come to light with the magic of the Japanese water flowers which bloom as you watch them. This is what is called instantaneous demonstration, but it is only that the word was spoken true, and the pattern which it set before infinite Mind was immediately made flesh, or visible. Some words are slower to germinate, but sooner or later all of them come to life and bear after their kind.

Now, do not throw in a handful of wheat and then cover the ground with seeds of vicious plants and expect to have a golden harvest. Be persistent in sowing good words, words of power and happiness, words of strength and courage, words of prosperity, and presently the harvest will come. Some people spend fifteen minutes a day in the silence, saying good words and thinking grand and noble thoughts, and then come out and spend the rest of the twenty-four hours in the most vicious of thinking.

The more we understand of the power of right thinking the more we will be able to make these words appear before us clothed in demonstration.

One thing we must learn as we go along is that if we have been in the habit of condemning either ourselves or others, we are to stop this action short. "Neither do I condemn thee" does not only apply to our misjudgment of others but also has to do with ourselves. We are learning that we must drop off the "poor worm of the dust" attitude and take on the glorious "Sons of God" idea. We must stop degrading the temple of the living God by calling it old, worn-out, sick, crippled, or ugly and begin to praise it and to outline upon it beautiful and noble images. We shall hold in thought the model we wish to carve upon the block of stone before us.

We are all sculptors of our own lives, and the block of marble before us is given us for the purpose of carving out something beautiful. If your mind is filled with ugly and angular outlines, you will never produce a glory of beauty in your statue. If your thought is full of hate, criticism, sickness, and poverty, these you will surely trace on the stone before you, and this stone is to be the temple of the living God. This brings the power pretty close to you, doesn't it?" Well, the power is within, and the sooner you come to the full realization of the fact the sooner you will begin to change the design which you are carving on the marble in front of you.

Another thing—remember this: you are the sculptor, and you stand with chisel in hand ready to work, and as you stand, you are vested with infinite power, infinite beauty of design, infinite ability to accomplish any design that comes into your thought. You are the master workman. There is nothing which you cannot do.

Master workman, pause right here and see what is the pattern in your thought. What are your models, and do you need a new set? Again, if you are occupied with your block of marble, carving the design in your thought, you have no time to watch the next sculptor as he works and either envy or slander his work. While you look away, your chisel may slip, and you may make an ugly incision which will be hard to remove. Keep well to your task and quietly work out your design.

Remember that the word which is planted in secret will come to light, but do not trample it down or dig it up every few moments to see if it has germinated.

Plant it and leave it, watering it with the great, powerful words. My word "shall not return unto me void," for I have made my connection with the great storage house of infinite Mind. Keep it secret. As the seed needs the darkness to germinate, so your ideas and plans need the secrecy of your mind to germinate. If you call it from the housetop, you will dissipate all your energy, and the seed will die because it has been sapped of its vitality. If you discuss your plans with others before they have fully matured, then you will have the weeds of their wrong thinking to battle with.

Keep your work a secret. When it is ready for the world to know, it shall be so evident that no word from you will be necessary. How often have you known someone who told what they were going to do utterly fail in it and finally be angry if anyone asked them when they were going to do a certain thing. If the energy they had spent in telling and repeating this bit of news to another had been conserved and applied to the right channels of thought, they in all probability would have succeeded in accomplishing their desire and then would have been plenty of time to have told. Guard your work, commune freely with the Father within, for that is the Source of all power.

Praise every atom of good you see, both in yourself and others. Praise every atom of health and glorify the temple in which you are living. Remember, you are Spirit and not body, and the temple you inhabit is under your control. Remember that there is nothing which can in any way sidetrack you but your own thought about a thing.

Oneness

Perhaps you think you have already spoiled your block of marble and there is little hope of doing anything with it. This is a wrong thought, for the infinite Mind with which you can make direct connection can easily correct and erase any ugly designs and give you a new and fresh chance. Even marble becomes plastic under the touch of the infinite Mind.

Opportunity is never lost—it is only lost sight of for a moment. Remember, then, that you are master; that you have in your hands the Word, which is powerful and which will accomplish whereunto it is sent.

Remember, then, that from now on we are to watch the words, that no weak, idle words are included in our talk either of ourselves or others.

Remember that you are a sculptor at work and that you can chisel only what you see in thought.

Reversing

The reverse of a lie is the truth. The reverse of sickness is health. The reverse of poverty is wealth. The reverse of sorrow is harmony and joy. All these things, all these reverses, are going to be brought about in your life because we know that happiness is real and eternal and that unhappiness, discord, and poverty are unreal, hence they have neither power, place, nor permanence, because they are simply the result of evil, or wrong thinking.

We know now there is but one power, and this power if rightly used can be made to do anything necessary to bring into manifestation our desires, but when our desires are wrong, weak, sick, or bad, then the power is turned into these channels and produces after the patterns shown on the mount. Do not blame God for your condition. Look to the patterns you are holding up before you and see where the true fault lies.

This seems like a colossal statement, but the day is past when we creep along, page after page, trying to get at the meat of the truth. I am giving you plain facts in a plain, simple way, asking you to accept them until you find out they are false. You can put them to the most practical test at once, and if you find them wanting, do not go further.

For a little test work, let us try this simple thing. Suppose you are pitying yourself and your lot; suppose you feel like the whole world is all wrong, and as you go along the way with a heavy heart, you think your lot is the worst in the world. You cannot see any of the beautiful flowers along your way nor hear the birds nor catch the infinite harmonies of soul, until you suddenly pass a man in a wheelchair and at the corner meet up with a blind man and a little further on chance onto the deaf and dumb cobbler.

Suddenly the whole thought that you had before is reversed; you find that you have infinite things to be grateful for. What would any one of these unfortunates give to be standing in your place? Gratitude wells up in your heart. You have suddenly reversed all the downcast thinking, and you are actually counting your blessings and are happy.

Now, this is a very simple little example. You can try it any time you are downcast or unhappy. You will only have to walk two blocks to find out you are pretty well off. It will also bring to your mind the grand verity that what is true of this little test is also true of the more severe conditions which you are entertaining mentally, and you will find that by the reversing process you can, if you are persistent, overcome any untoward condition. Everything is thought, and thinking is the very life of both you and the universe in which you live.

Now, remember this simple little point: thought is the only action in the universe. You have to think before you can do the slightest thing, though perhaps you have become so used to it, so habituated to doing certain things, that it is unconscious thought—but just the same, it is thought.

At first, the job of reversing is not so easy. Perhaps you are suffering from a condition of poverty, and when you reverse the order and say, "I am wealthy because I am Spirit and one with the Father of all wealth, the source of all supply," it seems like telling a bald-faced lie. But never mind how it seems. Don't for one minute, after you have taken your stand at reversing, let the idea of poverty take the floor again, no matter if it seems actually to be a solid and concrete fact. The reason it seems to be a fact is that you have thought it so long and so hard that you have solidified it and made it something which appears awfully real, and you have held the poverty mold in front of your eyes so long that you reproduce the design without being conscious of it. Start the reversing process, and you will begin to see a slight stir at once, and ways and means will begin to open up for you that you have not dreamed of.

Now, do be reasonable about these things. There is nothing which is going to drop down from the skies into your lap as you meditate upon wealth. No unreasonable things do I ask or call to your attention, but as you know you are one with the Father within and that all things are open unto you, new ideas will come to you which, if acted upon, will open channels of supply for you that will meet your every need.

Do not be afraid to follow the leadings of your heart after you have gone into the silence and listened attentively for the still small voice, as all ways will open up for the accomplishment of your desire. "Be not afraid, only believe."

One of the greatest difficulties that people encounter in making the Word flesh is that they lack singleness of purpose. They change their ideas with such rapidity that they constantly have a changed pattern before the mind, and as a result, it can reproduce nothing. Another serious mistake that is made is the attitude "leave it with God" and holding the mind a perfect blank without desire, wish, or formulated plan. This may be all right for the introduction of love, faith and hope, but if you have some desire which has to come forth in the material, you will have to hold a design exact and complete before the mind constantly, in order that it may be reproduced and brought forth in completeness.

If you sit down to draw and try to draw a circle while you hold the image of a square in your mind, what kind of a picture will you bring forth? Probably a hexagon— neither a square nor a circle. This is true if you desire today to be a carpenter and change it tomorrow to a preacher.

Reversing

You must have singleness of purpose and take your positive stand. Decide just what you want and then outline perfectly in your mind and each day hold the pattern up, knowing that the Father will open the way for the accomplishment of it, for you are making your connection with the infinite Source of all power, and that nothing can keep you from accomplishing your desires.

When the eye is single, then the whole body or temple or workshop is full of light. Now, if you will take a check over your desires and see that you are not changeable, but hold fast to one set plan and pray to the Father in secret, you will see the manifestation come forth openly. There will be plenty of light to guide you, and your dream will be accomplished.

Once you have taken the reversing method, turn not back, neither give way to doubt because of appearances.

In Australia, there is said to exist a white ant which eats the wooden frame of a house entirely away, many times unbeknownst to the owner of the house. All of a sudden, the house will collapse and go to the ground in a heap. Perhaps the brick or cement house stood in perfect order this morning, and five minutes later it is a heap of dust and debris.

This is the way the reversing works. Perhaps you cannot see a single bit of difference in the problem, and perhaps it stands day after day just like it did, but if you are faithful and refuse to accept the lie, one morning it will collapse and disappear. Just like the walls of Jericho—they did not fall the first time, neither the second, nor the third, nor yet the fourth, but one morning they crumbled away and were no more, and that is the process of persistent reversing. Finally the model before the mind has become a habit of thought, and the mind goes to work to reproduce almost unconsciously what it desires. Believe this or not, it is the truth, and you can prove it if you will only be a little patient.

When you reverse the lie and cling steadfastly to the fact that you are one with the Father within, which is Spirit, and that right thinking is the Father within, you are sending out these seed thoughts into a very fertile soil, and presently the crop will astonish you. New interests will come to you; new powers will manifest themselves in your behalf, and you will find that through some little thing or other, perhaps it will be ever so small, the deed is done and you have overcome the condition which you have been reversing.

I call to your attention the story of *Arabian Nights* where two wealthy men had a discussion as to the best way of making a man wealthy. One said to give him a good big start, the other said to give him a little seed. So they agreed to try it on a poor tentmaker.

The first man gave him two hundred pieces of gold and told him there was his start to independence. So overcome with his sudden wealth was the poor tentmaker that he rushed at once to the market and purchased a large piece of meat for himself and family. He put the hundred and ninety pieces of gold in his turban as he hurried home to his wife, after having spent the ten pieces for food. On the way home a raven, smelling the fresh meat, flew down and tried to snatch it out of his hands with his sharp claws. In fighting him off, the raven, by some chance or other, got his claws hooked in the turban and flew away with the turban, money and all.

When the rich man returned, he found the tentmaker in the same condition as before, and when he told him about the raven, the rich man laughed, but said to him, "Here is another two hundred pieces." The tentmaker was again overjoyed, and this time he hid one hundred ninety pieces in an old jar of bran as he went to the market to buy some food for the family. During his absence, his wife met up with a street vendor who was buying old vessels, and she sold him the jar of bran for a few coppers. Imagine the man's plight when he told his wife what was in the bran.

When the rich men returned, the first one admitted that his idea had failed, so the second one took his chance. As he came along the way, he had picked up a piece of lead, a sinker to a fishing net, which he presented to the tentmaker saying, "This is the beginning of your fortune, use it carefully and well."

The tentmaker thought he was making light of him and put the sinker on the shelf and went on with his work. That night a neighbor, who was a successful fisherman, came and knocked on the tentmaker's door and asked if he had a bit of old metal that he could use for a sinker; he had lost one and the shops were closed, and he could not get anything at that hour in the night. Suddenly the tentmaker thought of the piece of lead and gave it to the fisher, who said to him, "For this I shall give you the very first seine that I draw—if it be a hundred fishes or if it have nothing, the first net shall be yours."

The next morning he presented the tentmaker with one huge fish which was the first catch. The fish was so large that they could not possibly have used it, so they decided to sell the whole thing at the market. When they did, it was the first extra money they had ever had, and so they invested it in some canvas and hired another tentmaker to help make another tent. As soon as the increase from this sale was made, it was invested again, and gradually out of the little lead sinker, the poor tentmaker became a large manufacturer of tents and a rich man.

The story is this—that from the tiniest seed thought, if well planted and tended, can grow the mightiest demonstration. From the tiny acorn the oak springs, and the pattern of it lies slumbering in the acorn, perfect and intact. There is no doubt as to what the outcome will be when you plant the acorn—it is going to bring forth an oak tree, and if it is properly cared for, it will make a giant of the forest. Or it can be trampled underfoot because it is first small and of no particular value. The tiny seed of your faith, when planted, will not send up a mighty oak with one bound, but it will push up a slender plant which, if you watch and guard carefully, will at last be the sturdy oak of your need. The thing that tramples the demonstration into the ground is the fact that we allow the wrong thinking process to come in and destroy our molds of good.

Take your positive stand today and reverse the lie as it comes to you. No matter what it says, reverse it and keep reversing it right in the face of the most evident facts to the contrary, and presently you shall see results which will startle you.

Suppose you are ill; suppose you have a certain diseased condition of the body. When you plant the first seed thought of good, when you know that you are Spirit and not matter, that you are one with the supreme Source of all life, then you are beginning to prepare the ground for a crop of perfect health, and nothing can keep the demonstration from you except you turn back. The way is not difficult. It is not impossible but is just a matter of keeping up the reversing process.

Such an affirmation as "Everything which pertains to me and my affairs is well and good right now," repeated and thought over, will do wonders in a short time. For right thinking is all there is to the divine Mind, and wrong thinking all there is to mortal mind—they are one and the same thing, merely used or misused.

You shall make your decision today whether you will continue to misuse this force or power for evil results or whether you shall start the principle of reversing into action and turn again and be saved from the evil of your thinking.

Like attracts like, you well know. You cannot expect to attract wealth if your mind is full of poverty. You cannot expect to be happy when your mind is full of wretchedness and inharmony. You cannot expect to move an inch if you positively know within yourself that you cannot move an inch.

I have often heard it said, "That is just my luck" when some evil seems to overtake a person. Of course it is just their luck, for they have claimed it. How could they expect it to go to anybody else? Their mind has attracted it and held it, and it has come unto them. "Loose him and let him go." Loosen all these old dead beliefs about a personal luck, a personal devil, etc., and you will see that they were only hanging around because you were holding them to you, and for no other reason were they there.

Another thing as we go along the way: when we start the reversing, let us cut out the malice, hatred, judging, condemning, and criticizing others. We have no time for this now. Let them alone. "What is that to thee? follow thou me." Follow the new pattern which you have set before the clean tablet of your mind and watch that you keep your own eye single. Pay no attention to what your brother is doing, saying, or advising—follow the inner voice and be saved.

About the Author

Walter Lanyon was highly respected as a spiritual teacher of Truth. He traveled and lectured to capacity crowds all over the world, basing his lectures, as he said, "solely on the revelation of Jesus Christ."

At one point, he underwent a profound spiritual awakening, in which he felt "plain dumb with the wonder of the revelation." This enlightening experience "was enough to change everything in my life and open the doors of the heaven that Jesus spoke of as here and now. I know what it was. I lost my personality; it fell off of me like an old rag. It just wasn't the same anymore."

His prolific writings continue to be sought out for their timeless message, put forth in a simple, direct manner, and they have much to offer serious spiritual seekers.

Walter Clemow Lanyon was born in the U.S. on October 27, 1887, and he passed away in California on July 4, 1967.

Made in the USA
Middletown, DE
03 October 2023

40096958R00057